CATECHETICAL CRAFTS FOR THE LITURGICAL YEAR

CATECHETICAL CRAFTS for the LITURGICAL YEAR

LEE PALENCAR

TWENTY-THIRD PUBLICATIONS
twentythirdpublications.com

TWENTY-THIRD PUBLICATIONS
1 Montauk Avenue, Suite 200, New London, CT 06320
(860) 437-3012 » (800) 321-0411 » www.twentythirdpublications.com
**A DIVISION OF
BAYARD, INC.**

ISBN: 978-1-62785-228-9
Library of Congress Catalog Card Number:
Printed in the U.S.A.

CONTENTS

INTRODUCTION

Through all the years I've been helping young children learn about their faith, I've found again and again that the right activity, the right craft, can make the lessons come alive for them. In this book I offer some of the most effective and creative of these crafts to tie your lessons to the liturgical year and the church's seasons. They are simple to make (you don't have to be a craft expert!), with clear instructions and easy-to-find materials. I hope you and those you teach enjoy creating these meaningful crafts that are sure to enhance your lessons.

Lee Palencar

1

Encouraging self-awareness, introducing God, who loves us and makes each of us uniquely ourselves.

God Made Me Self-Portrait

God is love! He made each of his children beautiful and unique! Your students have unique looks and personalities, likes, dislikes, feelings, and reactions. And each is lovingly created by their heavenly Father! Each of us is an individual. Even twins! This creation of a self-portrait is often an awakening to this concept of self as individual. It's also a wonderful opportunity to create a safe environment where each student's individual uniqueness is accepted.

PRAY

Father, I celebrate each student's growing self-awareness as your unique and loved creation. Help me convey the love you have for them, in your name. Amen.

WHAT YOU NEED

- ☐ 9" x 12" white paper
- ☐ pencils
- ☐ crayons
- ☐ mirrors, if possible

WHAT TO DO

Hold a class discussion with your students about each one's unique qualities. Ask them to think about what skin, hair, and eye color each has. Are they missing teeth? If you have mirrors, have them look carefully at their faces before they draw. (Refer to Image 1 as an inspiration for students.) Pass out a 9" x 12" piece of white construction paper and a pencil to each student. Then tell them to begin drawing their faces as their loving Father created them. Remind them to think about details such as face, eye, nose, and lip shapes, how their eyebrows and eyelashes grow, and, if they smile, how their teeth grow out of their gums.

Then pass out the crayons for students to add color.

When they are finished, be sure to celebrate by having each student hold up his/her self-portrait as the rest of the class applauds. Display all self-portraits, if possible.

Image 1

ANGELINA, KINDERGARTEN; USED WITH PERMISSION.

I Am Part of God's Family Wreath

Love is relationship. While each of us is God's individual creation, we are meant, in his loving plan, to live and love together in community. Immediate families are our first community; our connections then broaden to include neighbors, schools, and churches. As we mature, we realize we belong to the eternal family of God. Express this unity with a neverending circle wreath made with overlapping individual hand tracings joined together in love.

PRAY

Loving God, enlighten me so that I might expand my students' horizons by introducing the concept that each individual is connected to another, and to all, through you, who are neverending Love. Amen.

WHAT YOU NEED

- ☐ large bowl, plate, or platter
- ☐ smaller plate or saucer
- ☐ poster board in any color
- ☐ pencils
- ☐ child-proof scissors
- ☐ glue
- ☐ construction paper in assorted skin tones
- ☐ *optional:* white construction paper and skin tone crayons.

WHAT TO DO

Prepare the wreath by tracing the large bowl onto the poster board. Then trace the smaller plate inside the center of the larger circle, creating a donut shape. Cut it out. *(See Image 1.)*

After students select a skin tone color of construction paper, pass out pencils. Provide assistance as students trace a single hand, keeping their fingers apart. Remind them to hold the pencil so that the eraser is pointed to the ceiling, producing a more accurate-looking hand shape.

Pass out scissors for students to cut out their traced hands.

Students bring their paper hands to you to glue onto the wreath, with the fingers symbolically outward, as if reaching out to embrace and include others in God's family. *(See Image 2.)*

You may choose to write students' names on the hands, truly making each a part of God's family!

Then roll pieces of masking tape and adhere to the back of the wreath to secure it on a door, wall, or window.

You may also choose to write "I Am Part of God's Family" on a piece of construction paper to display with the wreath.

Optional: Students trace hands on white construction paper and use a variety of skin tone crayons to color.

Image 1

Image 2

OCTOBER ▪ ORDINARY TIME

Foster an understanding of our guardian angels, who love and guide us all through our lives.

Guardian Angel Be at My Side Card

God gives a gift to each of his children—an angel who loves and offers guidance throughout our lives. Help children understand that they can pray to this angel for protection and help in making good and loving decisions. Suggest that the Guardian Angel Be at My Side card be put in a place where the students will be able to see it often, perhaps while brushing their teeth or during nighttime prayers. Or it might be placed in a central family location where the whole family can see it.

PRAY

My Jesus, lead me to inspire my students to envision themselves as children of their tender, loving Father, who so generously gave them a special guardian of love. Amen.

WHAT YOU NEED

- ☐ patterns of the face, wings, and body
- ☐ tagboard, cereal box cardboard, or card stock
- ☐ construction paper in skin tones for the angel faces, yellow for the "star" angel wings, and an assortment of colors for students to choose from for the angel body
- ☐ child-proof scissors
- ☐ glue
- ☐ pencils
- ☐ *optional:* craft stick (popsicle stick)

WHAT TO DO

Prepare patterns for your students by tracing shapes onto something sturdy like tagboard, cereal box cardboard, or card stock, and cut them out. *(See Image 1.)*

Precut construction paper of each size and color so students can easily trace the pattern without waste.

Students trace each shape onto the appropriate color of construction paper with pencils.

Students carefully cut each shape from the traced construction paper.

Instruct students to put a spot of glue on the center of the yellow star.

Then have them place the triangle on top of the star with the longest part of the star for the upper wings and the smaller part for the bottom of the wings. Press to seal.

Now students glue the circle for the head, overlapping the tip of the triangle. *(Refer to Image 2.)*

Each student may write his or her first name at the bottom of the angel to personalize. Or students may choose to name their angels.

Each student may glue his/her angel onto a craft stick making it easier to hold, like a puppet.

Image 2

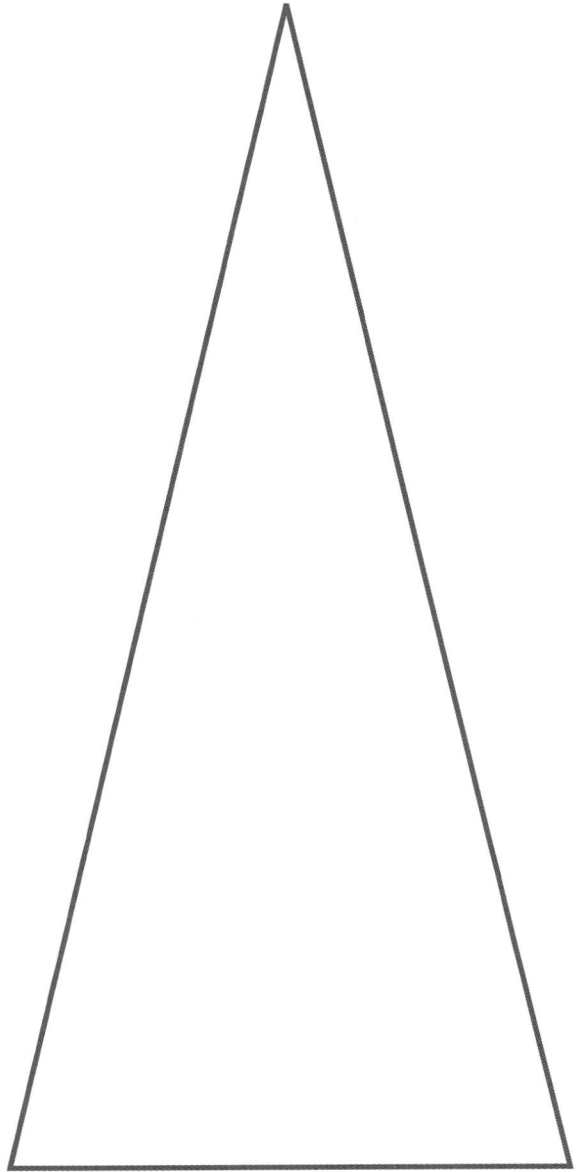

Image 1

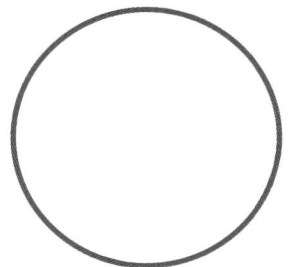

NOVEMBER ■ ORDINARY TIME

Introduce St. Thérèse of Lisieux and her Little Way of doing little things with great love in order to help children understand how consequences work and to grow in holiness.

Good Deed Beads

St. Thérèse of Lisieux counted her little sacrifices and her good and loving actions on a string of beads similar to this one. Throughout each day she reflected on her thoughts and actions, both loving and not so loving, and moved the beads to count—forward for good, and backward for not so good. She did this to know herself better and to show more love for our loving Father, God. It didn't matter how small her good thoughts and actions were, because they were done for love of God and his people.

Help your students practice good and loving acts with these colorful beads, moving a single bead forward for each good thought and deed, and backward for the not so good. Remind them that love often requires sacrifice. The better we come to know ourselves, the better we can grow in love.

PRAY

Holy Spirit, help my students become aware of the consequences of their thoughts, words, and actions, for ourselves and for others. Amen.

WHAT YOU NEED

☐ one 6" chenille stick (pipe cleaner) per student
☐ 12 pony beads per student

WHAT TO DO

Give each student a 6" chenille stick and a single pony bead. *(See Image 1.)*

Demonstrate threading the bead and placing it about an inch from one end. *(See Image 2.)* Then fold the end of the stick over the bead and twist it on itself to secure the bead in place. *(See Image 3.)*

Give each student another pony bead, or if students are capable, ten pony beads, to thread, one at a time, onto the long end of the chenille stick until they stop at the secured bead. *(See Image 4.)*

Have each student place the twelfth pony bead on the unsecured end, leaving about an inch so that the chenille stick can be folded over and twisted on itself to secure it in place. *(See Image 5.)* And this completes the Good Deed Beads as shown in Image 6.

Tell students to keep the Good Deed Beads handy in a pencil pouch or pocket throughout the day, and when they smile instead of ignoring a student, or help someone pick up dropped books, or sit next to someone who looks lonely at lunch time, a bead should be moved to the other side.

Stress honesty by reminding them that if they are unkind to a student or sibling, or disobey a teacher or their parents, they are to move a bead backward for each thought, word, or action.

When all ten beads have been moved because of sacrifices or loving acts, the Good Deed Beads are simply flipped to begin again.

Help your students transform this from a short-lived fad into a lifelong habit that increases virtues and growth in holiness. Ask students at each class meeting to share a single act of loving kindness with the rest of the class. Remind them this is not a time to brag but to share ideas and encourage each other in love.

Image 1

Image 2

Image 3

Image 4

Image 5

Image 6

5 NOVEMBER ▪ ORDINARY TIME
Practice giving thanks for our immediate family and the family of our church in community.

Holy Family Placemat

The Holy Family is our model for our own families. Just as we eat meals together, so Mary and Joseph sat with Jesus to share their meals. Imagine sitting at the table with Mary and Joseph, thanking God together in prayer, passing dishes to each other, having conversations about the day, complimenting Mary on the delicious food. Meals eaten together forge loving bonds between family members and strengthen relationships with Jesus. Encourage your students to use their placemat at family meals as a reminder that we are to try to be as much like Jesus' family as we can.

PRAY

Sweet Jesus, help me create visual images of you sitting at the dinner table with your mother and father, saying grace and sharing meals, so that I may help my students and their families relate to you in loving thanks. Amen.

WHAT YOU NEED

- ☐ patterns of the plate, spoon, fork, and knife
- ☐ tagboard, cereal box cardboard, or card stock
- ☐ 9"x 12" construction paper in assorted colors
- ☐ pencils
- ☐ child-proof scissors
- ☐ glue
- ☐ *optional:* scrap construction paper in assorted colors
- ☐ *optional:* markers

WHAT TO DO

Prepare by tracing the patterns *(see Image 1)* onto tagboard, cereal box cardboard, or card stock and cutting them out.

Hold a discussion about the Holy Family and your students' families. Students love to share family stories! Ask them about their funniest family meal, perhaps a holiday dinner with a silly aunt or funny cousin. Maybe a camping trip with a meal around a campfire and how that differs from being at home around the table.

Have students select construction paper colors for their plate and utensils.

Pass out pencils and the patterns. Ask the students to trace the plate and utensil patterns onto construction paper.

Students then cut them out.

Pass out one 9" x 12" piece of construction paper for each student and have, or help, them arrange the cutout plate and utensils on it and glue them securely.

Students may write with markers on their new placemats. Suggestions include: "My family is like Jesus' family," "I love my family," or "My family rocks!"

You may laminate each placemat or cover it with clear adhesive-backed vinyl so they can be wiped down after each meal.

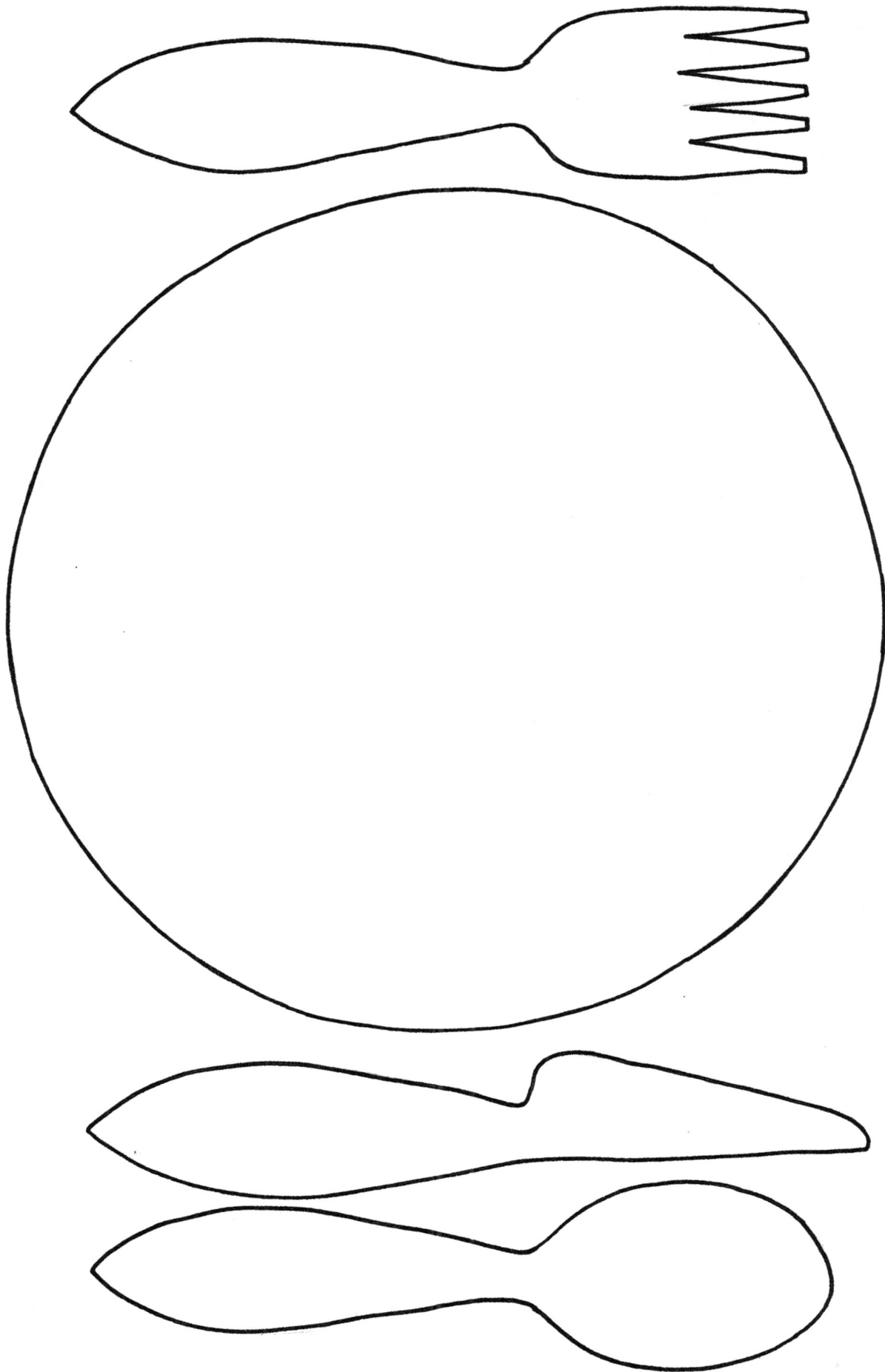

6

Introduce Advent as a time of patient waiting—through the celebration of faith, hope, joy, and love—for Jesus to come.

Advent Candles Stand-Up

Jesus is coming! Each Sunday of these four special weeks we light a candle as we wait patiently for Jesus, the Light of the World, to be born. The first Sunday of Advent, we light a purple candle in hope. The second Sunday, we light another purple candle in faith. The third Sunday, we light a pink candle for joy. And on the fourth Sunday, we light the last purple candle in love.

Students make a personal connection to this season by displaying and positioning an accordion fold of Advent candles so that the appropriate one is revealed each week. This is also a wonderful opportunity to teach the importance of waiting patiently for God to reveal his plan for each of us. Increasing trust in God is necessary for relationship with him.

PRAY

Giving Father, give me the means to encourage my students to detach from the constraints of time and to replace it with trust in Jesus, who is coming, Emmanuel, God with us—you with us. Amen.

WHAT YOU NEED

- ☐ patterns for the candle and flame
- ☐ tagboard, cereal box cardboard, or card stock
- ☐ pink, purple, and yellow construction paper
- ☐ child-proof scissors
- ☐ glue
- ☐ 9"x 12" white construction paper
- ☐ **optional:** yellow crayon or marker for home use

WHAT TO DO

Prepare for this activity by tracing the patterns for the candle and flame onto something sturdy, like tagboard, cereal box cardboard, or card stock and cut out. *(See Image 1.)*

Precut the construction paper to the pattern sizes to lessen waste.

Give each student a piece of purple construction paper and have him/her trace the candle pattern with a pencil.

Each student repeats this two more times with the purple precut paper, and one time with the pink construction paper.

Each student now has four candles traced onto construction paper: three purple and one pink.

Now give each student precut pieces of yellow construction paper and have them trace the flame pattern four times with a pencil.

Have each student cut out his/her own candles. When finished, cut out the flames.

Have students fold the 9" x 12" white construction paper into fourths to create an accordion, then open and lay flat. You may prefold for your students.

Each quarter is for a single candle to be glued onto it. Then students glue a flame above each candle. When done, refold into an accordian. Each

Sunday, students "unfold" to reveal the appropriate candle for that Sunday in Advent. *(See Image 2.)*

Optional: Students may trace the flame onto the white construction paper and each week at home color it yellow with a crayon or marker.

Students may write the words, Hope, Faith, Joy, and Love, one on each candle.

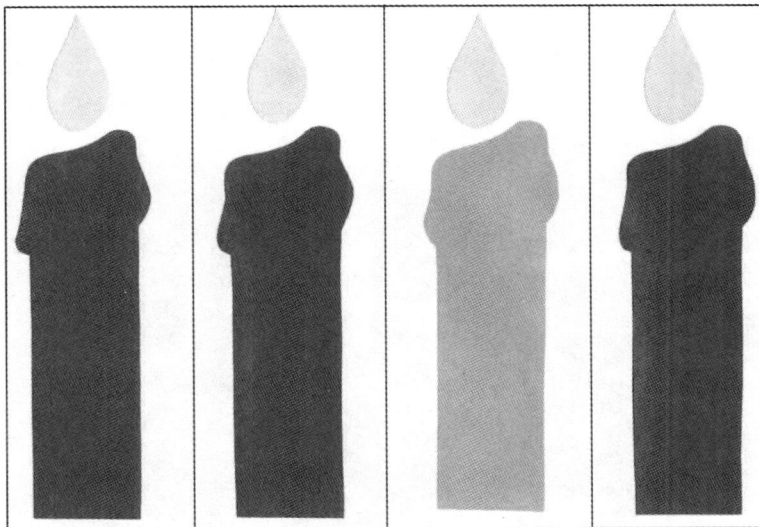

Image 2

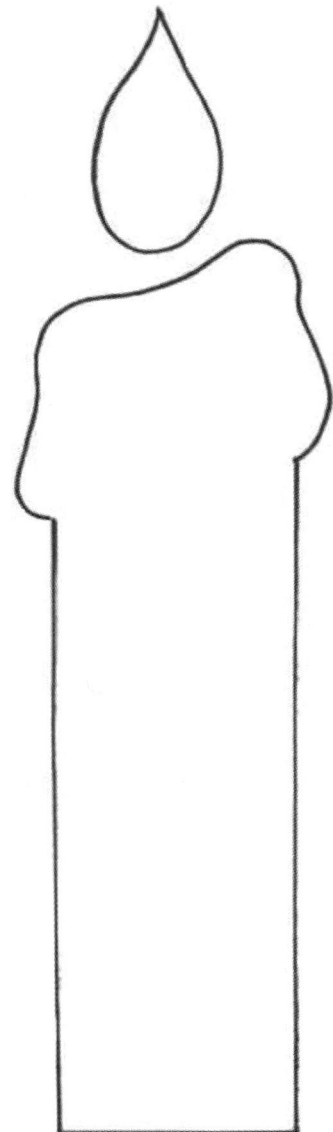

Image 1

DECEMBER ▪ CHRISTMAS

Celebrate the birth of Jesus as students are made aware of the contribution of each person present at this miraculous event.

Nativity Set

The Nativity of the Lord (Christmas) celebrates God entering into our world as one of us. Make this time even more wondrous by having your students create their own nativity sets to display at home. Or create one as a service project to donate to a children's hospital or nursing home. Mary, the Mother of God, St. Joseph, the earthly father of Jesus, the Baby Jesus, the shepherd, the three wise men, and two sheep make up this adorable scene.

PRAY

Holy Breath of God, guide me to show my students how extraordinarily miraculous it is that your love for us would inspire you to become a little, tiny baby. Amen.

WHAT YOU NEED

- [ ] 8 cardboard toilet paper tubes per set
- [ ] 1 photocopy of the eight character outlines per set
- [ ] assorted construction paper
- [ ] crayons, markers, or colored pencils
- [ ] child-proof scissors
- [ ] glue

WHAT TO DO

Prepare by photocopying one character outline page per set then cutting out each character on the thin, black outline. (*See Image 1.*)

Also prepare each toilet paper tube by gluing a piece of construction paper over it, cut to size, commonly 4" x 6". Use a variety of colors.

Have students color the characters with crayons, markers, or colored pencils.

Pass out covered toilet paper tubes, one for each character.

Students glue characters on the toilet paper tubes, lining them up at the edges, until the Nativity Set is complete and ready for display. (*See Image 2.*)

Image 2

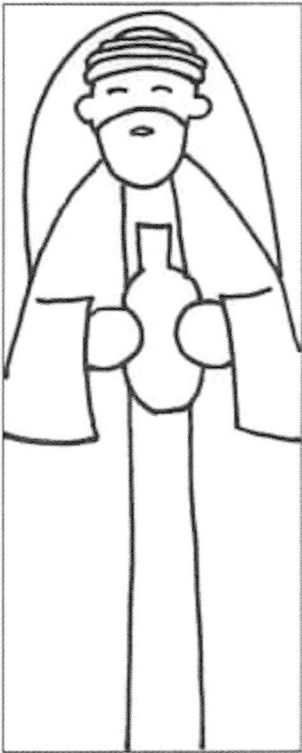   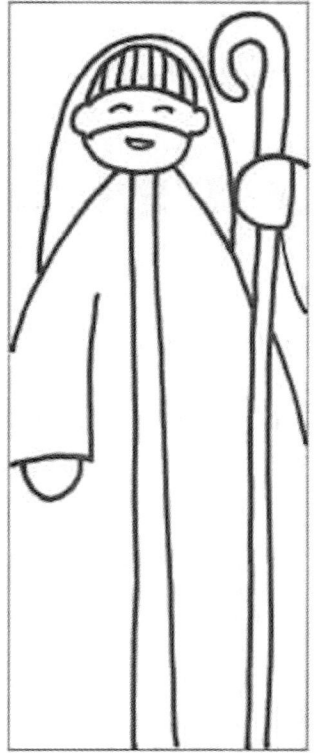

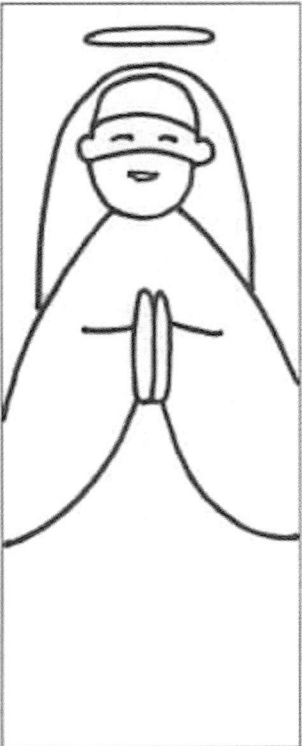 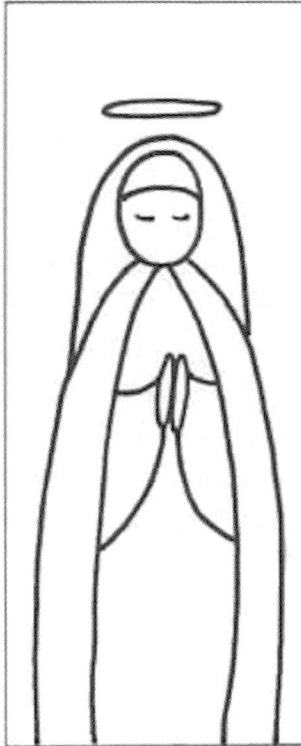 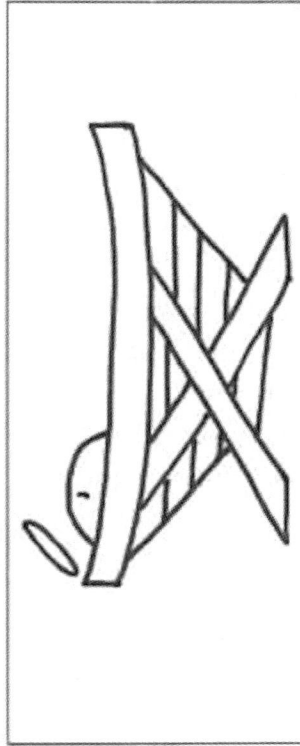 

JANUARY ■ ORDINARY TIME

Introduce different types of prayer: praise, petition, gratitude, and repentance.

Letters to Jesus Display

Jesus is Emmanuel, God with us, in his church and in each of us. The sooner that students learn to say "Yes!" to a relationship with Jesus, the more they will feel comfortable talking with him in prayer.

There are many types of prayers: praise (giving glory to God), petition (asking something of God), gratitude (expressing our thanks to God), and repentance (asking forgiveness for the times we have not responded in love). This activity is a way to encourage students to talk to Jesus and to develop a lifelong relationship in prayer.

PRAY

Holy God, assist me in drawing my students into the kingdom of heaven through prayer— conversation with Jesus—through both talking and listening. Amen.

WHAT YOU NEED

- ☐ patterns for the teacher-created mailbox and flag, using construction paper in any colors for entire classroom display
- ☐ brass fastener so the flag can pivot freely, or glued-on button as shown, or simply color a circle to indicate the rivet
- ☐ display board may be a bulletin board, chalk board, foam core presentation board, a cardboard box side or whatever is large enough to hold your student letters

- ☐ 8½" x 11" white paper cut into quarters, one for each student
- ☐ pencils
- ☐ markers
- ☐ glue

WHAT TO DO

Prepare ahead of time a single display board of the mailbox and flag that will be shared by the entire class using the pattern pieces. *(See Image 1, which includes the pattern pieces and final display.)* You can also cut a rectangle for the support pole of the mailbox. Use a marker to indicate the curve of the mailbox. Write "Jesus" on the mailbox.

After discussing types of prayers and reciting an example of each with your students, they can begin writing their letters.

Give each student a piece of paper. Remind them to keep their prayers to a single topic.

When students have completed writing their prayers, tape, staple, or pushpin each around the mailbox. Fold letters for privacy if students prefer.

You may want to have students write to Jesus periodically, adding to or changing the letters on display, using the liturgical season as a prompt.

If your students don't know how to write yet, have them whisper their prayers to you, and you act as secretary. Or you can write different prayers on the board for students to copy. The happy point is to get them conversing with Jesus!

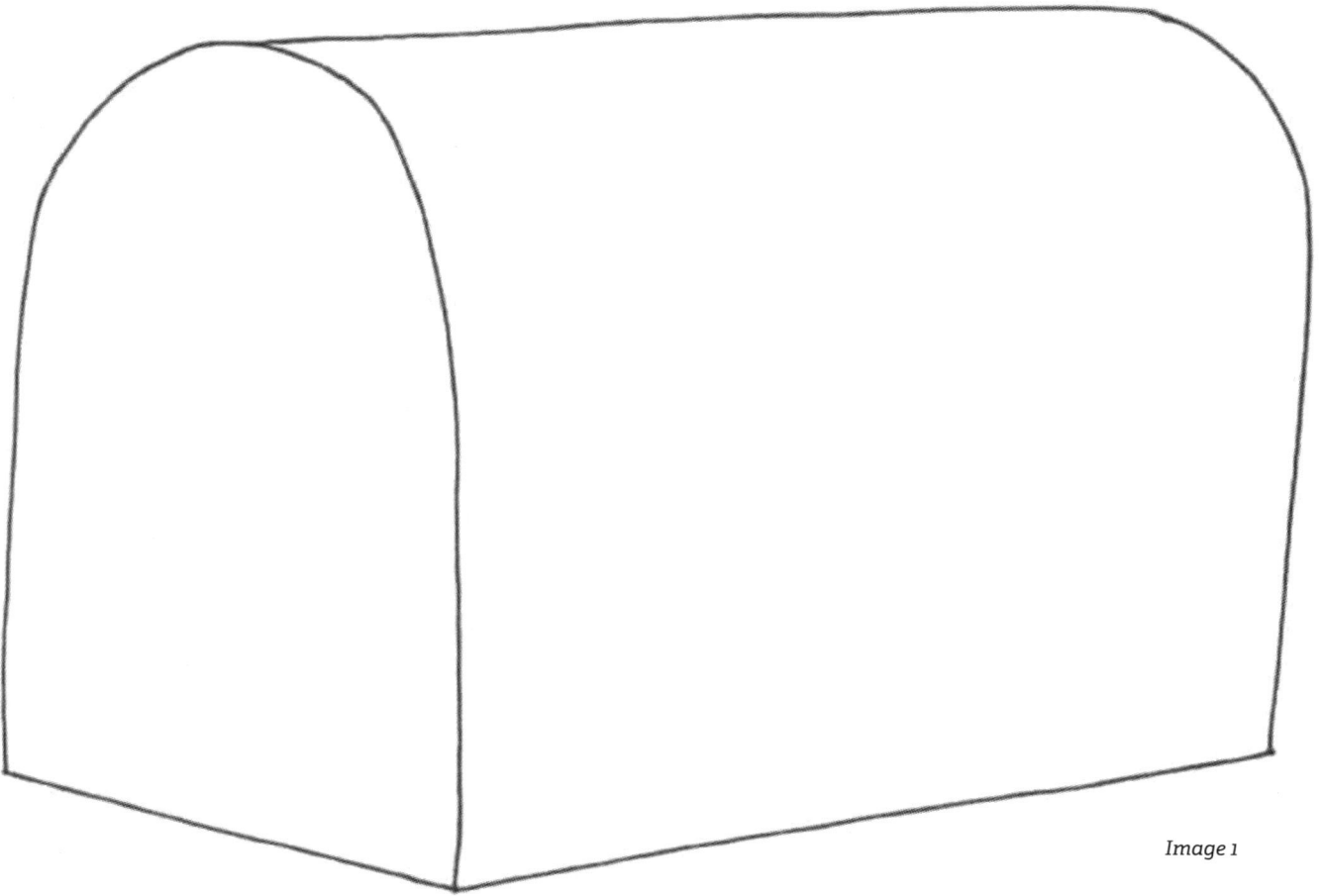

Image 1

Image 2

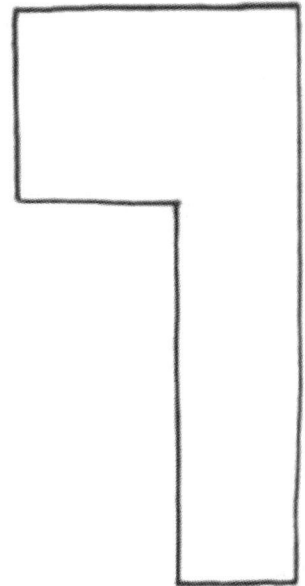

Celebrate the mystery that Jesus gives himself to us in the Eucharist, the sacrament of Holy Communion.

Eucharist Wall Hanging

*The sacrament of the Eucharist is, according to the **Catechism of the Catholic Church**, "the source and summit of the Christian life." We are invited deeply into the Christian life through the regular celebration of the sacrifice of our Lord Jesus in the Eucharist.*

Making wall hangings of the images of the Eucharist, the host and chalice, is a great activity for those preparing for their First Communion.

PRAY

Jesus, my love, provide the words for me to express this mystery of your Body and Blood as our spiritual food as we find in you the source and summit of our lives. Amen.

WHAT YOU NEED

- [ ] patterns of the chalice and host
- [ ] tagboard, cereal box cardboard, or card stock
- [ ] 9" x 12" felt in assorted colors for the chalice, host, and background
- [ ] yarn, one 12" length per student
- [ ] pencils
- [ ] child-proof scissors
- [ ] standard single hole punch
- [ ] glue
- [ ] permanent markers
- [ ] *optional:* jewels or beads to decorate chalice

WHAT TO DO

Prepare by tracing the chalice and host patterns *(see Image 1)* onto tagboard, cereal box cardboard, or card stock and cutting them out. Also, for each wall hanging, cut two 1½" x 9" strips out of tagboard, cereal box cardboard, or card stock; then punch one hole on each end of half of the strips. *(See Image 2.)*

Pass out felt for the chalice and have students trace the chalice pattern onto it with a permanent marker. Pass out the felt for the host and have students trace the host pattern onto it with the marker.

Students cut out the chalice and the host from the felt. Provide assistance as needed.

Then pass out one 9" x 12" piece of felt per student for the background.

Students spread glue on the backs of both the chalice and host (the back will be the side with the permanent marker visible) and then place them onto the 9" x 12" felt background, pressing to seal.

Have students glue the prepunched strip to the top back and the un-punched strip to the bottom back, as shown in Image 2. These two strips will add stability and weight, allowing the wall hanging to hang properly.

Position the hole punch over the prepunched holes in the top strip only. This makes it easier to punch through the felt. Students thread one length of yarn through the holes and tie knots to secure. *(See Image 3.)* Voilà!

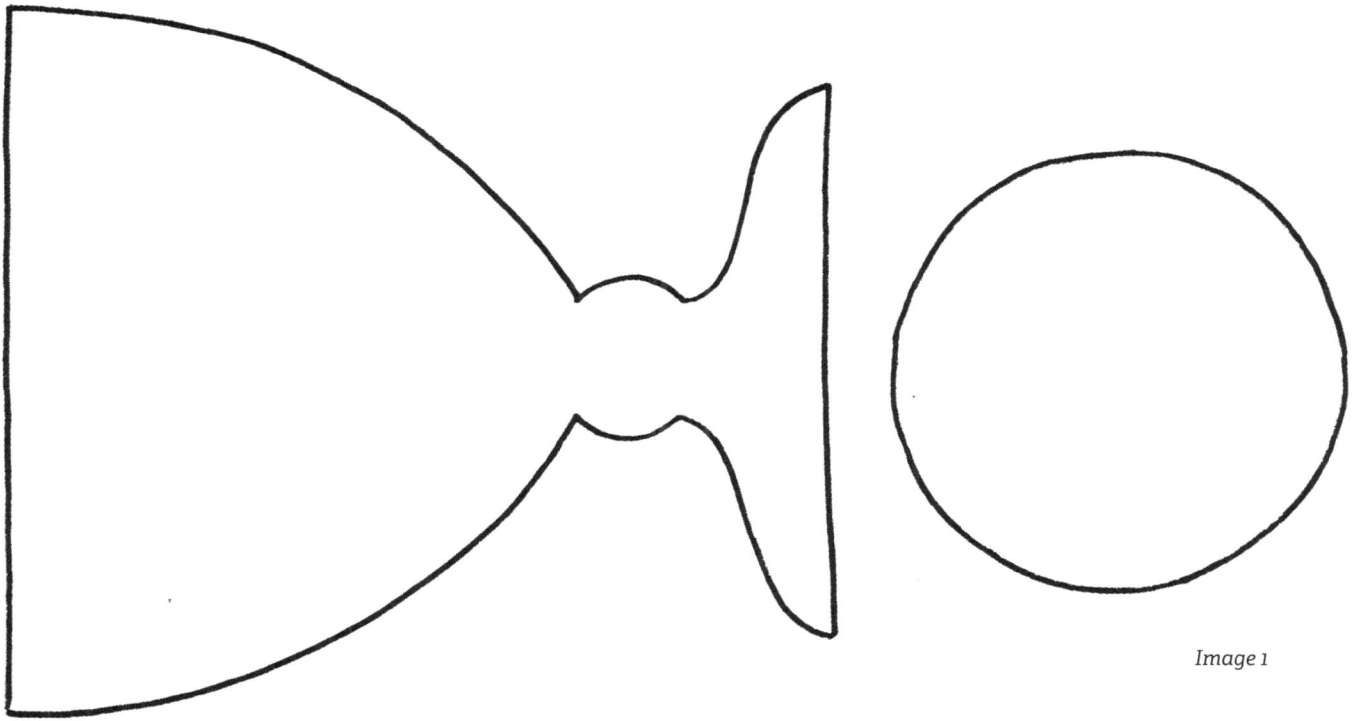

Image 1

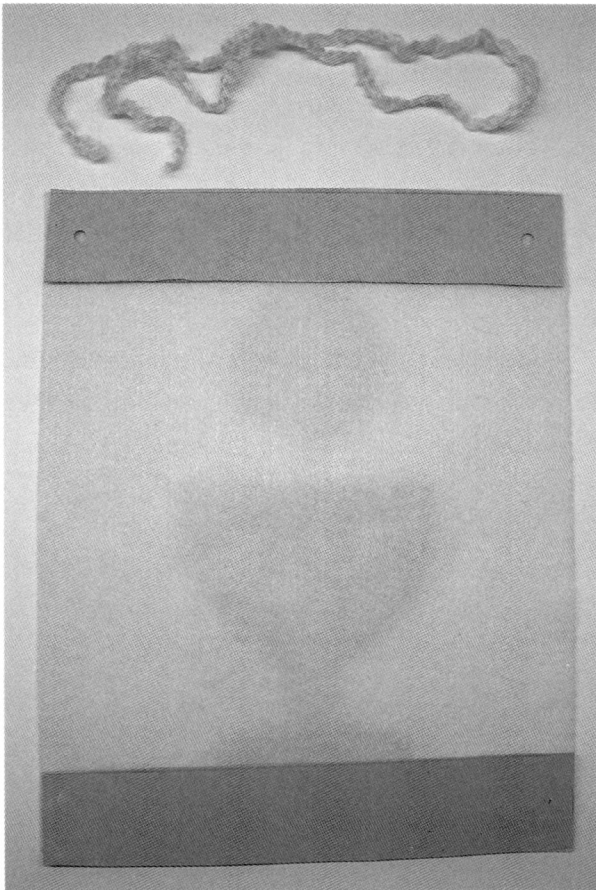

Image 2

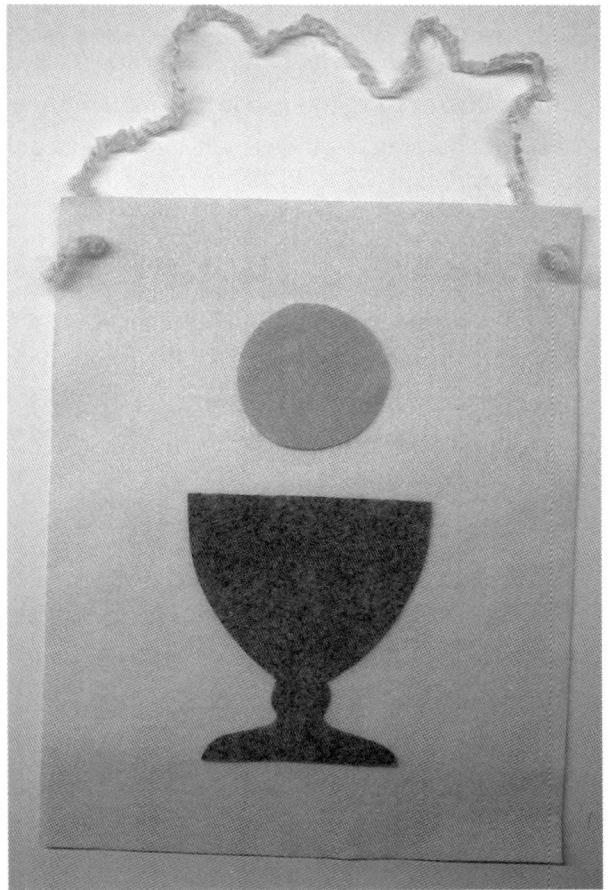

Image 3

MARCH ▪ LENT

Celebrate St. Joseph, the church's model of fatherhood, and acknowledge fathers and positive male influences by making this gift of love.

St. Joseph Bracelet for Fathers

The model father, St. Joseph, opened his heart, mind, and will to God. Your students can recognize their fathers or male influences in their lives by giving them a handmade bracelet to honor them.

You may enhance this lesson by having your students share favorite stories of their experiences with their fathers or male influences. This too is a great way to celebrate them.

PRAY

Spirit of God, guide me as I help my students see the importance of the good and loving men in their lives who are helping to guide them, like St. Joseph, on the path to you. Amen.

WHAT YOU NEED

- ☐ plastic canvas cut to 12 squares by 54 squares
- ☐ roughly two yards of yarn per student, any color
- ☐ one darning needle per student (blunt end and large eye)
- ☐ child-proof scissors

WHAT TO DO

Give each student a precut piece of plastic canvas, and a darning needle prethreaded with about 10" hanging from the eye of the needle.

Tell students to pull the needle up from the bottom through the space at the outer edge of the bracelet, leaving about a two-inch length of yarn. Tell them they are going to outline the entire bracelet. *(See Image 1.)*

Then, they insert the needle down from the top into the very next space. Repeat until the entire bracelet is outlined. Tie a double knot using both ends of the yarn on the back. Cut off extra yarn but keep the remaining yarn threaded for the next two steps. *(Refer again to Image 1.)*

Have students insert the needle in and out of two holes at the middle of the short end of the bracelet and double knot at the plastic mesh, leaving two lengths of yarn about five inches long. Repeat on the other end. These are the ties that allow the bracelet to be secured and adjusted in size to the father's wrist. *(See Image 2.)* You can decorate with symbols, such as the cross, shown on the bracelet.

You could invite the fathers and male influences into your classroom, where the students present their bracelet gifts in a happy ceremony!

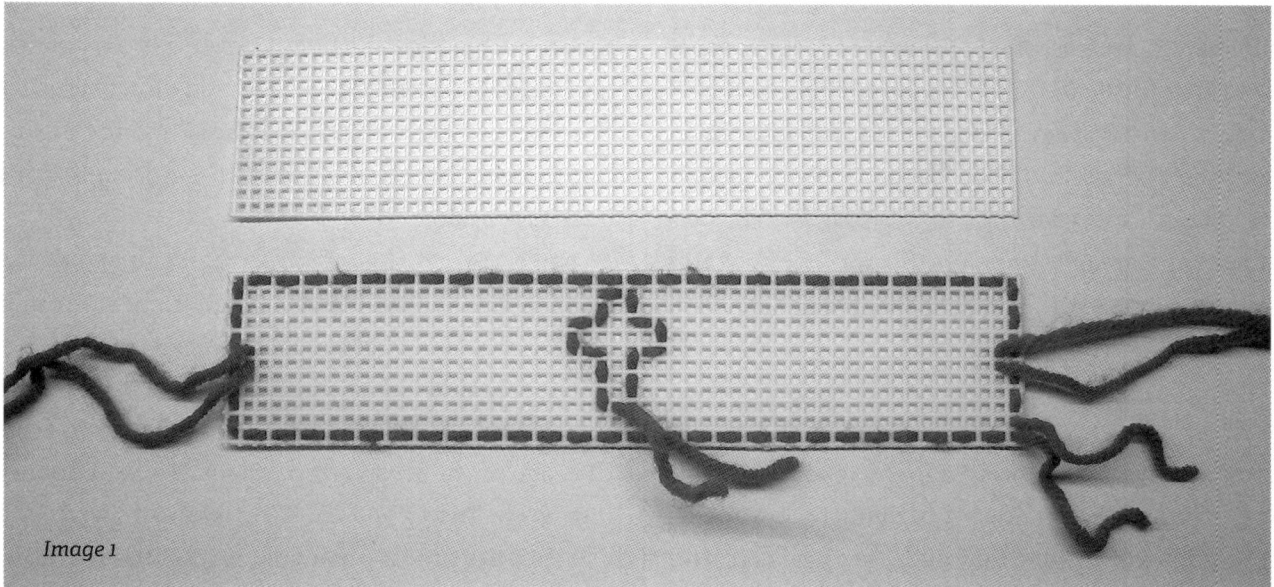

Image 1

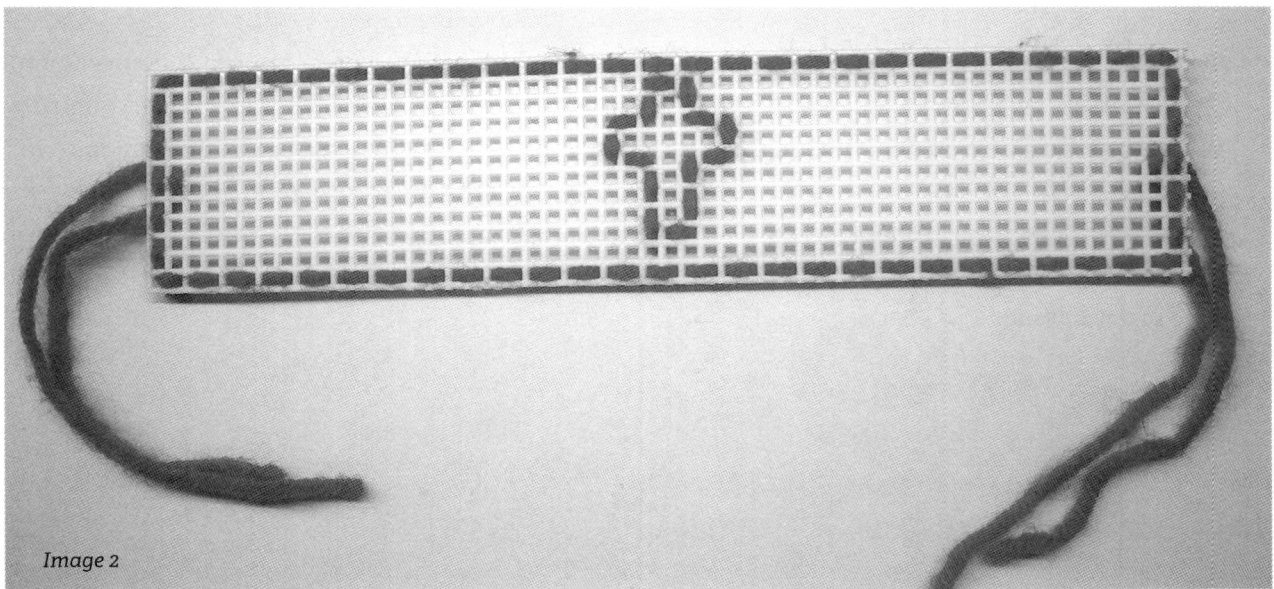

Image 2

11

MARCH ■ HOLY WEEK

Introduce the symbol of the Holy Cross, a reminder of Jesus' love and sacrifice in dying for us. It shows us that we can always trust in him.

Cross

The cross of Christ, a concept students often find difficult to understand, symbolizes the love that Jesus has for us in dying for us. His love is never-ending. Learning reverence for this holy reminder is reinforced by having students make their own personal crosses that they can display in their bedrooms during Lent, hang on the family Christmas tree, or place near the front entrance of their homes.

PRAY

Loving Jesus, accompany me as I teach this mystery of your tremendous act of dying for us, and let this symbol of a real event open our hearts to you. Amen.

WHAT YOU NEED

☐ plastic canvas
☐ roughly one yard of yarn per student, any color
☐ one darning needle per student (blunt end and large eye)
☐ child-proof scissors

WHAT TO DO

Using the plastic canvas, cut out one cross per student as shown in Image 1. Finished dimensions for the crossbar will be 4 by 12 squares, and for the upright, 4 by 22 squares. Trim off the little nibs for a neat appearance.

Next, thread the yarn through the eye of the darning needle, pulling about ten inches through. Give one to each student along with a single cross.

Direct students to pull the needle up through the space at the very top, second square in from the edge of the cross, telling them to leave between four to six inches of yarn. *(See Image 1.)*

Students are to push the needle down and up each square going around the perimeter of the entire cross. *(See Image 2.)*

When they get back to where they began, pull off the needle then trim the yarn to the same length as the original yarn piece. *(See Image 3.)* Tie a double knot to secure. *(See Image 4.)* Now tie a double knot in the end of the two long pieces forming the hanger. *(See Image 5.)* The cross is now complete.

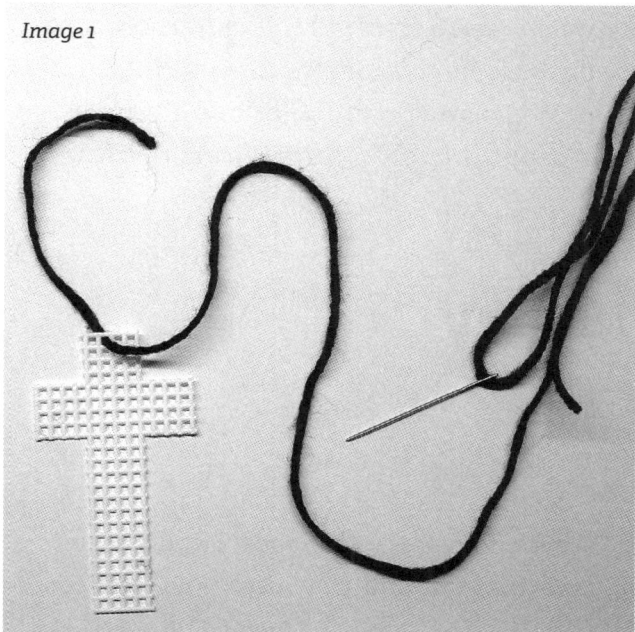

Image 1

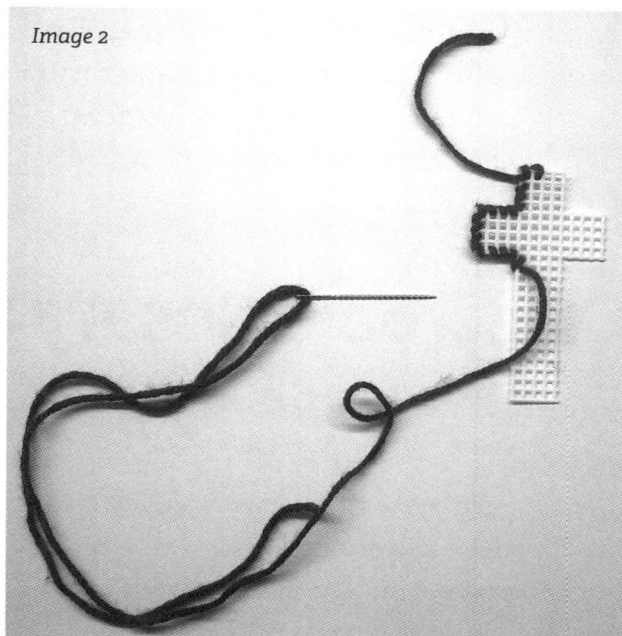

Image 2

Image 3

Image 4

Image 5

12 | APRIL ▪ HOLY WEEK

Recite the prayers of the Rosary, a gift from Mary, our Mother, the Queen of the Rosary, as a class-community after each student contributes to creating this classroom rosary display. While praying the Rosary daily is encouraged, this blessed time of Holy Week is appropriate for contemplating specifically the Sorrowful and Glorious Mysteries, helping students move more deeply into this beautiful prayer form during this liturgical season.

Classroom Rosary Display

The Rosary is a gift of prayer from Mary, Our Mother. Said privately or in groups, this is a powerful and meditative type of prayer that can become a permanent part of your students' prayer lives.

In this project, students not only say the Rosary together bead by bead, but create it together, bead by bead. This is an excellent project demonstrating how small pieces can join to become a whole.

PRAY

Jesus, show me how to inspire my students to love this gift of prayer given to us by your very own Mother. Help us unite as a community in our saying of this prayer together. Amen.

WHAT YOU NEED

The shapes and sizes for your rosary will be determined by the size of your display. In the example shown in Image 1, three-inch circles were used for the Our Father beads, and two-inch circles were used for the Hail Mary beads. Yours may differ.

- ☐ tagboard, cereal box cardboard, or card stock to make your own patterns
- ☐ construction paper in assorted colors
- ☐ pencils
- ☐ child-proof scissors
- ☐ glue
- ☐ *optional:* foam core 3-panel display board, poster board, bulletin board, door, wall, etc.

WHAT TO DO

Prepare by making a small circle pattern, a larger circle pattern, a cross pattern, and a triangle pattern out of tagboard, cereal box cardboard, or card stock and cut them out.

Students create the smaller beads by tracing the pattern with a pencil onto construction paper then cutting them out. You will need 53 smaller circles to complete a rosary.

Then have students cut out the bigger beads by tracing that pattern with a pencil onto another color of construction paper and then cutting them out. You will need six larger circles to complete a rosary.

Have a student trace the cross pattern and the triangle pattern out of another color construction paper and cut them out.

Once the beads, triangle, and cross have been made, begin assembling onto the display. Do not adhere until all pieces are positioned properly. *(See Image 1.)* Enjoy this special prayer time with your students.

Image 1

| ### APRIL ▪ EASTER
Praise and reflect on how we hope in Jesus, the Second Person of the Trinity, rising from the dead and giving us eternal life, with this large-format holy card.

Resurrection Holy Card

Three days after his crucifixion, death, and burial on Good Friday, Jesus rose from the dead on Easter Sunday, defeating death for all of us. The Resurrection Holy Card is a reminder for students to never give up hope and always trust in Jesus. Encourage them to display this holy card in their homes to remind them that Jesus loves them forever.

PRAY

Father, allow me to let your light shine through me to these students in my care so that they feel your love mingled with mine. The risen Christ is our hope. Help me instill this within them so that they will always call on him in everlasting hope. Amen.

WHAT YOU NEED

☐ image to color

☐ 9" x 12" construction paper in assorted colors cut in half to 6" x 9"

☐ crayons, markers, or colored pencils

☐ glue

☐ *optional:* precut yarn and a hole punch

WHAT TO DO

Prepare by photocopying Image 1 for each student. Pass one to each student and give them access to crayons or markers and let them color the image of the risen Jesus, God the Father, and the Holy Spirit as they are inspired to.

Pass out one 6" x 9" piece of construction paper to each student along with the glue. Students glue the colored image of Jesus onto the construction paper, leaving a border of construction paper to act as a "frame." *(See Image 2.)*

Optional: hole punch at the top through the construction paper, then thread precut yarn through, tying into a knot, providing a method of hanging this image in students' homes.

Image 2

Image 1

14 | MAY ■ EASTER
Introduce the concept of the Third Person of the Trinity, the Holy Spirit, symbolized as a dove.

Holy Spirit Mobile

The Holy Spirit can be very mysterious to children and adults. It can be difficult to envision a spirit. We have some images mentioned in Scripture to depict the Third Person of the Trinity: breath, wind, and a dove. Your students may connect most easily with the beautiful white bird that is also represented as the dove of peace.

Matthew 3:13–17, provided below, provides wonderful imagery for students. Though Jesus does not need to be baptized, he models for us the perfect human being. The dove is introduced here as the symbol of God's Holy Spirit.

THE BAPTISM OF JESUS

Then Jesus came from Galilee to John at the Jordan to be baptized by him. John tried to prevent him, saying, "I need to be baptized by you, and yet you are coming to me?" Jesus said to him in reply, "Allow it now, for thus it is fitting for us to fulfill all righteousness." Then he allowed him. After Jesus was baptized, he came up from the water and behold, the heavens were opened [for him], and he saw the Spirit of God descending like a dove [and] coming upon him. And a voice came from the heavens, saying, "This is my beloved Son, with whom I am well pleased."

(*NEW AMERICAN BIBLE REVISED EDITION*)

PRAY

Father of love, I ask for the Holy Spirit to fill me with his love and guidance as I introduce the concepts of sin, forgiveness, and the symbolism of the dove to my students. Amen.

WHAT YOU NEED

- ☐ air-dry clay
- ☐ small metal paper clips, one per sculpture
- ☐ precut yarn or strings in appropriate lengths for your display
- ☐ small paintbrush
- ☐ *optional*: clothes hangers

WHAT TO DO

Show students Image 1 and tell them each one of them is going to make a small bird similar to what they see in Image 1. Each one will be unique. Ask them to listen for the Holy Spirit to inspire them as they work. You can choose to demonstrate how to create a simple bird form and then let them begin after you pass out roughly a quarter to a third of a cup of air-dry clay to each student.

Once the bird is formed, show students how to make "eyes" by pushing the end of the paintbrush on either side of the bird head about 1/8" deep.

Then pass out one paper clip to each student and demonstrate how to push one end of the paper clip into the back of the bird leaving half of it exposed to become the hanger. *(Refer again to Image 1.)*

Let the bird sculptures dry completely.

Students thread the yarn length through the opening of the paper clip, and then you can help them tie the ends around the bottom of the clothes hanger in a double knot to make sure they are secure. *(See Image 2.)*

You can hang clothes hangers from clothes hangers or stretch a long length of clothesline across your classroom and hang the clothes hangers on it. Or you may forgo the clothes hanger entirely and hang these beautiful sculptures on a tree, on push pins on a bulletin board, or from a dropped ceiling with hooks.

No matter how you display these sculptures, your students will be thrilled not only to see their creations, but to now have an image of the Holy Spirit to call their own.

Recite this prayer to the Holy Spirit by St. Augustine with your class:

Breathe into me, Holy Spirit, that my thoughts may all be holy. Move in me, Holy Spirit, that my work, too, may be holy. Attract my heart, Holy Spirit, that I may love only what is holy. Strengthen me, Holy Spirit, that I may defend all that is holy. Protect me, Holy Spirit, that I may always be holy.

Image 1

Image 2

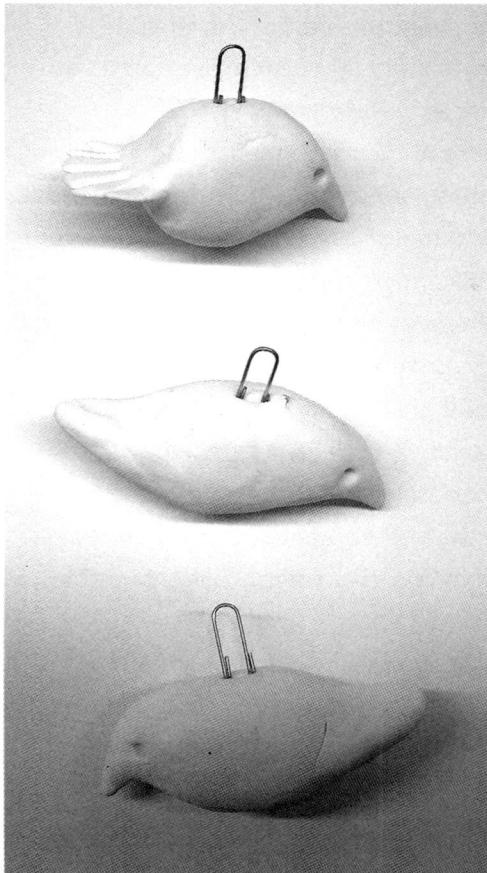

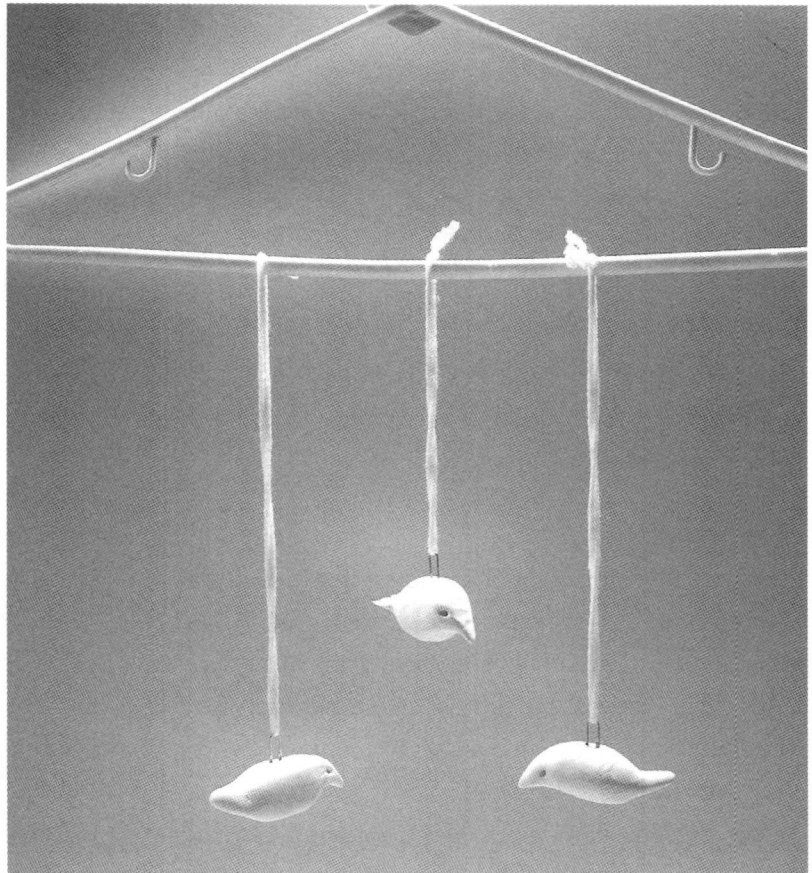

MAY ▪ EASTER
Celebrate Mary, the Mother of God, as Our Mother, too, the Queen of Heaven.

Crown for Our Blessed Mother, Mary

Traditionally, the Blessed Virgin Mary is crowned the Queen of Heaven in the month of May. This is a wonderful opportunity to have each student create a beautiful, personalized crown for your classroom statue of our Mother Mary during this warm and sunny time of year when flowers are blooming—as are our hearts for the Mother of Jesus.

PRAY
Jesus, help me draw my students to develop a devotion to your Mother, and our Mother, by inspiring them to create a beautiful crown just for her. Amen.

WHAT YOU NEED
- [ ] chenille sticks (pipe cleaners)
- [ ] pony beads and buttons making sure holes are big enough for chenille stick to fit through

WHAT TO DO
Prepare by wrapping a chenille stick around the head of your classroom statue of the Blessed Virgin Mary. This will serve as the measure of the chenille sticks you will cut, one for each student. You should have a good inch overlap to secure the ends once the beads are threaded.

If you don't have a statue, use a soup can for sizing, then students' crowns can be displayed on a bulletin board or display board to honor our Mother for the month of May.

Give each student a precut length of a chenille stick as well as access to buttons and beads. Have them bend about one-half inch at a 90-degree angle on one end of the chenille stick so the buttons and beads won't fall off.

They need to leave at least a half inch empty on the other end to twist the ends of the chenille stick together to create a wreath. See Image 1 for a variety of wreath ideas.

Based on the number of students and how frequently you meet, change the wreath so all will have a chance to honor Mary with their wreaths. You can take this opportunity to teach them about processions, singing songs to Mary, or saying the Hail Mary, as you walk to place a new wreath on her head. A small piece of rolled tape can help secure it on her head. *(See Image 2.)*

At the end of May, students can display their beautiful wreaths in their homes as a holy reminder of the love they have for their heavenly Mother.

Image 1

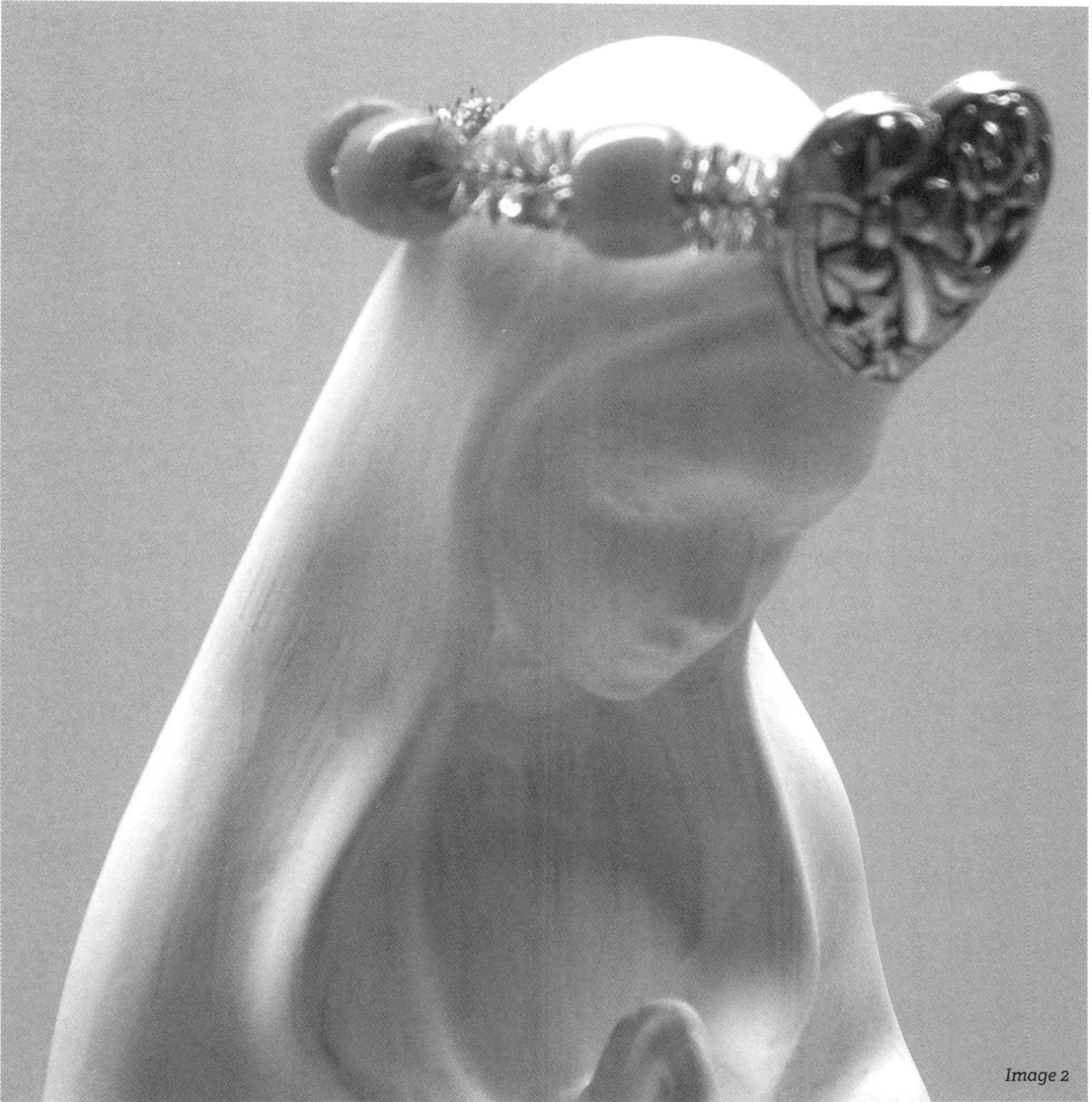

Image 2

Of Related Interest

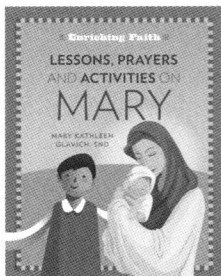

Enriching Faith
LESSONS, PRAYERS AND ACTIVITIES ON MARY
MARY KATHLEEN GLAVICH, SND

Help children develop a lifelong love for our Blessed Mother with these kid-friendly lessons and activities. Each lesson is reinforced with engaging activity sheets, plus background information for catechists and teachers.

72 PAGES | $14.95 | 9781627851459

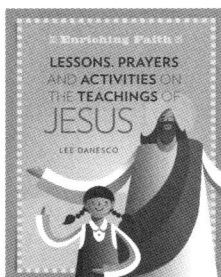

Enriching Faith
LESSONS, PRAYERS AND ACTIVITIES ON THE TEACHINGS OF JESUS
LEE DANESCO

Use this creative and engaging activity book to help you teach children in first grade and beyond about Jesus' teachings on loving God and neighbor.

72 PAGES | $14.95 | 9781627851046

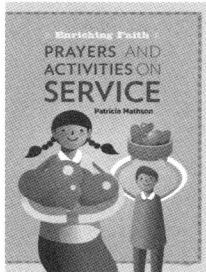

Enriching Faith
PRAYERS AND ACTIVITIES ON SERVICE
PATRICIA MATHSON

Help children make Christian service a way of life with this creative collection of outreach projects, learning experiences, and prayers.

72 PAGES | $14.95 | 9781585959372

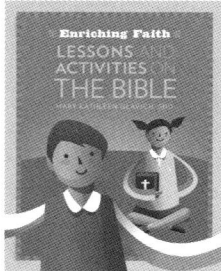

Enriching Faith
LESSONS AND ACTIVITIES ON THE BIBLE
MARY KATHLEEN GLAVICH, SND

Here are creative ways to introduce biblical lands and cultures, versions of the Bible, biblicalreference tools, and techniques for using Scripture as a basis for prayer.

72 PAGES | $14.95 | 9781627850278

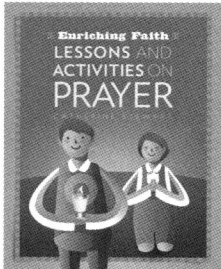

Enriching Faith
LESSONS AND ACTIVITIES ON PRAYER
CATHERINE STEWART

Here are dozens of fresh ideas to help your students see prayer in a whole new light.

72 PAGES | $14.95 | 9781585959471

TO ORDER CALL 1-800-321-0411
OR VISIT WWW.TWENTYTHIRDPUBLICATIONS.COM

TWENTY-THIRD PUBLICATIONS